MA$TERING RUG ECOMMERCE

Implement Proven Export Strategies *to* Expand *and* **Boost Sales**

AF663899

MA$TERING RUG ECOMMERCE

Implement Proven Export Strategies *to* Expand *and* **Boost Sales**

AMIT JAIN

Available on amazonkindle

Worldwide Published by

Pendown Press

PREMIUM BUSINESS PUBLISHER

PENDOWN PRESS LLP
An ISO 9001 & ISO 14001 Certified Co.,
Regd. Office: 3767A, Kanhaiya Nagar,
Tri Nagar, Delhi-110035
Ph.: 8130886000, 9650072927
E-mail: info@pendownpress.com
Branch Office: 1A/2A, 20, Hari Sadan, Ansari Road,
Daryaganj, New Delhi-110002
Ph.: 011-45794768
Website: PendownPress.com

Edition: 2026
Price: ₹ 399
ISBN: 978-93-7217-701-5

All Rights Reserved
All the ideas and thoughts in this book are given by the author and he is responsible for the treatise, facts and dialogues used in this book. Author is also responsible for the used pictures and the permission to use them in this book. Copyright of this book is reserved with the author. The publisher does not have any responsibility for the above-mentioned matters. No part of this publication may be reproduced, distributed, or transmitted in any form or by any means, including photocopying, recording, or other electronic or mechanical methods, without the prior written permission of the publisher and author.

Layout and Cover Designed by Pendown Graphics Team

Table of Contents

Acknowledgements

This book is more than just a collection of strategies; it's a reflection of decades of shared effort, values, and lessons that shaped my journey in the Indian export industry.

First and foremost, I want to thank my parents, Nirmal Jain and Ila Jain.

You not only built a business from the ground up, but you did so with integrity, patience, and purpose. The values you instilled, of consistency over shortcuts, and relationships over revenue, are the real foundation of this book.

To Maya, my life partner, thank you for being the calm in every storm, the believer in every bold idea, and the silent force that holds it all together. Your strength makes my work possible.

To my children, Ananya and Advay, your curiosity, questions, and energy remind me why I must leave not just a business, but a blueprint for better futures.

To my core team at Weavinghands Rugs, across Panipat, Mirzapur, Bhadohi, Noida, and beyond, thank you for embracing change, learning systems, and helping shape a company that blends soul with structure. You are the real doers behind the scenes.

To the artisans who trust us with their work, your hands are magical. Your stories deserve stages. This book is, in part, a tribute to the ecosystem you quietly sustain.

To fellow exporters and friends who questioned, challenged, and sometimes even doubted me, your friction helped me polish my clarity. Every spreadsheet, system, and solution I've built is rooted in those conversations.

And to the new generation of exporters reading this: you are the next custodians of India's reputation. May you build with confidence, scale with ethics, and find joy in the journey. Thank you for trusting this book as part of that path.

Foreword

I've known Amit Jain for over a decade, not just as a supplier, but as a problem-solver, a systems-thinker, and a fierce advocate for doing things the right way.

In an industry where communication gaps, missed deadlines, and unclear costing are far too common, **Amit has stood out as someone who believes in precision without losing authenticity.**

We first worked together on a collection for the German market. The brief was complex: custom colors, tight packaging requirements, split delivery timelines.

Most suppliers would've hesitated. Amit didn't.

Not only did he deliver, but he built a backend system to track every step and gave us real-time visibility into production. That level of partnership is rare.

Over the years, I've seen him mentor other exporters, share costing templates with competitors, and sit with artisans to improve consistency, not because he had to, but because he believes the Indian rug industry deserves better.

This book reflects that belief.

It's not just a how-to manual. It's a window into the mind of someone who has seen the chaos and decided to organize it.

Amit's approach combines deep field knowledge with digital intelligence.

He respects tradition but isn't afraid to bring in technology to scale what works.

If you're an exporter, artisan-led business, or just someone trying to bring structure into your operations, read this. **More importantly, apply it.**

Because, as Amit often says, "The real freedom in business doesn't come from bigger orders. It comes from cleaner systems."

~ Sanja

Germany, A Delighted Client for 12 Years

Peer-Speak: From One Exporter To Others

I've been in the textile export business for over 18 years.

In that time, I've made every mistake an exporter can make:

- From quoting blindly to dispatching goods without approvals.
- From overcommitting to under-documenting.

When I met Amit through a mutual connection, I was intrigued by how calmly he spoke about processes, like costing templates, order flowcharts, and client handover kits.

At first, I dismissed it. "Yeh sab theory hai," I told myself.

But I was wrong. What Amit had built wasn't a theory. It was years of learning and experiences, structured and repeatable, laid out as easy-to-implement systems.

Implementing just 3 of his systems:

- A Product Master
- Sample Tracker
- And Production Sync Sheet

— changed my business.

- Our client's returns have dropped.
- My team stopped calling me 50 times a day.
- And I started enjoying the work again.

This book is the best thing Amit could have done for the Indian export community. It's like sitting across the table from someone who knows the chaos, but has found a way out and is now showing you the map.

If you're reading this, don't just read it. Use it.

Because no one teaches this stuff. Not the export council. Not the sourcing agents. Not even your buyers.

But Amit has. And now you can use it to grow with grace, not grind.

Ramesh

A Peer from Agra

Preface: The Handmade Rug Landscape From Random & Broken To System-Driven Wins

For centuries, India has been home to one of the world's richest traditions in handmade rugs. From the intricate knots of Kashmir to the bold weaves of Rajasthan and Uttar Pradesh, Indian rugs are not just floor coverings; they are stories woven in wool, silk, and cotton. Each piece reflects a lineage of craftsmanship passed down through generations, rooted in culture, patience, and artistic precision. With regional styles as diverse as the country itself, Indian handmade rugs are globally valued and desired for their durability, symbolism, and beauty.

Yet, despite this deep heritage, the handmade rug industry today stands at a crossroads, caught between legacy and modernity, and unfortunately, it is broken in many places.

Most small to mid-sized businesses operate without established systems.

- Decisions are made based on gut feel.
- Pricing is erratic.
- Artisans are exploited or underpaid.
- Clients are increasingly demanding transparency, traceability, and professionalism.

Regrettably, our industry is still stuck in outdated Excel files and offline workflows.

- E-commerce is misunderstood.
- Logistics are chaotic.
- And branding is often an afterthought.

Without digital transformation, we are setting ourselves up to be replaced by cheaper, machine-made alternatives.

However, it doesn't have to be this way, and we are proof of that.

We have addressed and solved these challenges by developing a lean but powerful system that anyone in this industry can replicate.

From automating costing and dispatch tracking to managing production through barcoded workflows, every weakness can be turned into a system. We use Shopify for our consumer-facing brand Pequra. We have built a full ERP-lite system on Google Sheets. We use WhatsApp catalogs and QR-linked invoices for global clients.

But more importantly, we use data + empathy:

- Understanding each product's lifecycle.
- Each artisan's capacity
- And each customer's pain point.

This hybrid model of old-world craftsmanship and new-age tech is our winning formula.

And with this book, it can be yours too, but only if you choose to take action.

Let me be clear: losing money in this business hurts. But losing time hurts more. Every week that you delay your business transformation, you are handing over the future to someone else.

Every rug you couldn't sell due to a lack of digital reach, every cancelled order due to unclear communication, every artisan payment delayed due to poor tracking is a cost of not modernizing.

The market will not wait. And if you wait, you will either burn out or phase out.

Don't let the legacy you inherited become a liability. Let it become your launchpad.

So, Who Am I?

Hello, My Name is Amit Jain.

I am a second-generation entrepreneur and published author, currently managing a legacy family business that began its journey in 1984 with a simple vision: to preserve and promote the rich tradition of Indian handwoven rugs.

Born into the textures, colors, and patterns of a carpet-weaving household, I absorbed the craft not just through looms and yarns but through the dreams and struggles of the artisans who created them. Over the years, I have transformed this inheritance into a purpose-driven, tech-enabled export and domestic brand that merges traditional craftsmanship with modern business systems.

As a second-generation exporter, I've lived through both the old-world charm and the new-world chaos of the rug industry.

Our family started with a few looms, a deep respect for craftsmanship, and the hope that Indian-made rugs would someday find a place in homes across the globe. Today, that dream is a reality, but not without its challenges. Over the past two decades, I've worked with clients in more than 43 countries, including sourcing agents, boutique brands, architects, retailers, and wholesalers. I've seen firsthand what excites them about Indian rugs… and what scares them.

It's not the product. It's the process.

They ask:

- Will the shipment be on time?
- Will the color match? Will it look like the sample?
- Is it ethical?
- What if it gets delayed at customs?
- Will someone even reply if there's an issue after dispatch?

I wrote this book to answer those unspoken questions. Not with sales talk, but with stories, systems, and real-world experience.

Because I believe that trust is built not through one good order, but through consistent, transparent partnership. This book isn't a catalogue. It's a conversation.

A behind-the-scenes look at how we work, what we believe in, and what global clients like you should expect when sourcing rugs from India, especially if you're doing it right.

My goal isn't just to run a rug business. It's to help Indian exporters like you build companies that are trusted, respected, and scalable without burning out.

I want to simplify sourcing for your clients while making fulfillment smoother for you.

This book is a bridge between your artistry and the systems you need to scale it globally.

Today, I'm not just running a rug company, I'm building a movement to empower artisans, scale ethically, and take handmade rugs to every corner of the globe.

However, as it happens in the life of almost every entrepreneur, the journey wasn't always smooth; I faced downfalls, too. The real downfall, however, wasn't a single moment of collapse.

It was a quiet but steady decline;

- Missed opportunities
- Increasing cancellations from clients
- Razor-thin margins due to overdependence on foreign buyers
- And the stress of handling everything manually.

Our team would spend weeks creating samples, investing in materials, only to face sudden PO withdrawals or quality complaints based on misunderstandings, not merit.

I realized we were running on legacy, but not on logic.

Our business lacked systems. Our clients had shifted online, but we hadn't.

That was the wake-up call. We weren't just behind on tech; we were losing control.

That realization became my turning point.

I decided to reinvent our business from the ground up. I didn't want to be a passive exporter; I wanted to be a global brand owner. I wanted to know who the end customer was, what they needed, and how to speak to them directly. So, I began exploring e-commerce, building websites, joining platforms like Shopify, Etsy, WordPress, learning about fulfillment, SEO, brand storytelling, all while reengineering our internal workflows using ERP-style systems SAP, Oracle, etc.

Finally, we built a system that doesn't require millions but some simple logic and knowledge. It wasn't easy, but it was liberating.

The past 25+ years were filled with trials, setbacks, late payments, and hard-earned lessons. I spent lakhs of rupees building websites that didn't convert. I ran ads that brought zero ROI. I partnered with freelancers who didn't understand our industry.

But each experiment added a layer to my understanding.

I started documenting every costing formula, mapping every product to its artisan, creating SKU-wise profitability, and building dashboards to monitor dispatches, returns, and sample status.

Slowly, I began creating a digital ecosystem: a smart backbone that could run our traditional business like a modern startup. What emerged was a blueprint not just for survival, but for scaling in a sustainable way.

Over the last 25 years, **I have worked with over 200+ global clients,** including wholesalers in Germany, boutique brands in the U.S., retail chains in the UAE, and interior designers across Europe.

We've shipped rugs to more than 43 countries and generated over $63+ million in revenue through a combination of traditional export, D2C, and e-commerce strategies.

We've helped over 500 artisans double their income, created job opportunities for rural women, and designed custom rugs for commercial spaces as well as homes.

What sets us apart is not just our product, but our process:

- Quality tracking
- Ethical sourcing,
- No child labour,
- And a deep respect for both design and delivery

My mission is to empower 1,000+ rugpreneurs, artisans, and small manufacturers to take charge of their future. I want to democratize the knowledge I've gathered, from exports to e-commerce, from barcode to branding, and turn it into a playbook for anyone passionate about building a globally respected, values-driven rug business. If I can do it with a small team and self-taught systems, so can you.

Why This Book & What Will It Do For You?

Over the years, I've met hundreds of fellow Indian exporters; some seasoned, some just starting out.

And one thing became clear:

While we excel in product and heart, most of us struggle with structure and scalability.

We rely on memory instead of systems. We negotiate on price instead of value. We repeat mistakes because we never had time to document our process.

And yet, we have world-class products.

What's missing is the roadmap.

This book exists because I believe it's time we stop depending on agents, trade shows, or sheer hustle, and start building businesses that work predictably, profitably, and proudly.

It's not a tech manual. It's not a spiritual pep talk either.

It's a grounded guide to help you:

- Understand what international clients truly expect
- Build tools that give you control over your margins
- Stop reinventing the wheel with every order
- Automate the parts of your business that exhaust you

If you're serious about building a rug business that lasts, one that your team respects and your buyers trust, **then this book will show you what took me 20 years to figure out.**

And if you're just starting? Even better. **You'll avoid all the mistakes I made along the way**

I work intensively with artisans, exporters, small business owners, and creative entrepreneurs in the handmade rug and textile industry.

Over the years, I've realized that even the most talented creators often remain invisible to the modern buyer, not due to a lack of product quality, but because of a lack of visibility, systems, and digital literacy.

Through consulting, coaching, and co-building tech-enabled business flows, I've seen firsthand how one shift, a e-commerce store, a better cost sheet, a barcode, or even a product video, can transform a traditional family business into a profitable, scalable brand.

Clients today expect speed, clarity, and trust. But most traditional businesses still rely on handwritten notes, Excel chaos, and WhatsApp confusion. Customers often face delayed deliveries, unclear pricing, unprofessional packaging, and poor post-sale support.

Even when a good rug reaches the buyer, there's no brand recall.

For B2B clients, the biggest frustration is the lack of systemization, no clean PI, no barcode-based tracking, and no clarity on who made the product or how to reorder.

These problems lead to lost orders, poor margins, and stunted growth.

I dream of an industry where handmade doesn't mean outdated.

- I want to see artisan-led businesses that proudly say: "Yes, we're small, but we run smart."
- I envision a world where rugpreneurs use digital tools without losing the soul of craft. Where customers worldwide can trace the story behind every rug they buy.
- And where the export-import game is no longer an elite club but a well-documented, system-driven business playground accessible to every honest maker.

That is why this book, due to constraints of time and logistics, I cannot be everywhere and reach everyone.

However, with a book I can reach a great number of people in a shorter time, thereby bringing velocity to my mission of serving.....

This book is not just a knowledge dump; it's a compact, result-oriented guide. Think of it like your business compass. With it, you'll learn to shift from being a doer to a system-builder. You'll stop being reactive and start becoming proactive. You'll understand how to attract premium clients, convert cold leads into warm relationships, and build lasting trust, all while preserving the magic of handmade.

We live in a world of collapsing attention spans and rising costs. Long coaching programs and endless webinars often overwhelm more than they help.

- This book was born from my desire to give you a shortcut, a structured, distilled version of 25+ years of mistakes, lessons, pivots, and breakthroughs.
- It will save you years of guesswork and lakhs of rupees.
- More importantly, it will fast-track your transformation from a service provider to a trusted brand.
- And that's what creates real velocity, not just in revenue, but in reputation.

Who Is This Book For & How To Use It?

This book is not written for rug buyers. It's written for the rug builders.

The entrepreneurs, exporters, manufacturers, and studio founders who are trying to bridge the gap between tradition and transformation.

If you identify with any of the following, this book is for you:

- You run a small or mid-sized rug export business and feel stuck in outdated processes.
- You've inherited a family-run operation but want to modernize it for global relevance.
- You manage sampling, costing, and dispatch yourself, and feel exhausted.
- You want to build an online brand but don't know where to begin.
- You've been let down by trade shows, agents, or inconsistent buyers.

This is a handbook for Indian rug exporters and artisan-led businesses who want to:

- Create clarity in pricing and production.
- Streamline fulfillment, QC, and communication.
- Build a brand that commands trust, not just discounts.

Whether you're in Panipat, Jaipur, Mirzapur, or Bhadohi, this book is for you if you want to turn your traditional rug operation into a modern, scalable, values-driven business.

This is not just a book. It's your permission slip to think bigger. You have the product. You have the passion. What you need now is the process. Let this book be your mentor, your blueprint, your mirror.

Don't just read it, use it.

This book is not meant to be read once and shelved. It's designed to be used, like a toolkit, a compass, and a mirror.

If you're feeling overwhelmed with client orders, costing confusion, or dispatch chaos, this book will show you how to regain control.

If you're just starting out and unsure how to deal with international buyers, this book will help you lay a solid foundation.

To make the most of it, here's how to use this book:

1. **Read in order,** each chapter builds upon the mindset and methods of the last.
2. **Pause and reflect,** apply what's relevant before moving forward.
3. **Print & implement tools,** especially if you've downloaded the Rugpreneur Toolkit.
4. **Circle the problems you relate to,** talk to your team or coach about them.

5. **Highlight insights;** the ones that stick are the ones worth repeating.
6. **Revisit when needed;** every growth stage reveals new relevance.

This book is not just a guide. It's a shortcut. Let's make it work for you, your team, and your clients.

Your rug business deserves more than survival. It deserves scale, success, and soul. Let's begin.

Even before you start reading the actual transformational content shared in this book, I have a gift for you.

To go deeper and apply the learnings from this book with focused guidance, visit **www.theamitjain.com** to book your free strategy session today.

CHAPTER 1

Busting the Myths That Keep Rug Businesses Small

Before we talk about anything else about the handmade rug business, we need to clear the air. Right at the onset, this chapter tackles the two most common and most limiting myths that keep artisans and exporters stuck in cycles of stress, stagnation, and self-doubt.

These myths aren't just false, they're expensive. They cost you clarity, time, and trust from buyers. But once you bust them, you'll unlock a simpler, smarter path to sustainable growth, one that doesn't require fancy software or million-rupee makeovers. Just a shift in mindset, and the willingness to act on what actually works.

Myth 1: Digital is not for me

The biggest thing holding you back isn't capital, competition, or even the market; it's a myth. A costly one.

It is a myth that has kept countless businesses stuck in outdated habits, thinking that systems and structure are reserved for big corporations with IT teams and massive budgets.

And I'm going to start by dispelling it right now:

Once you shift that, everything else follows.

Many handmade rug businesses operate in what I call organized chaos.

Every process, from costing and sampling to dispatch, is driven by memory, experience, and reactive decisions.

While this worked in the 1990s and early 2000s, it is no longer sustainable. Today's market is driven by precision, visibility, and speed.

If you can't show the customer what you made, what it costs, and when it's reaching them, in one clean interface, they will go to someone who can.

That's the real challenge

All of this can be addressed by embracing simple digital systems; however, **the biggest and costliest Myth & Mistake in our industry is this:**

"Digital is too complex."

Most artisans and small businesses think that going digital means:

- Expensive CRMs
- Paid subscriptions
- Or hiring coders.

The truth is, the best systems I've built were **on free Google Sheets, using simple logics and workflows that even a teenager could manage.**

The problem isn't technology, it's mindset.

And this book will help you shift that.

Myth 2: "To Grow Fast, I Must Change Everything."

Many rug entrepreneurs believe that scaling requires radical change:

- New teams
- Big loans
- Expensive consultants
- Large warehouses
- And fancy marketing.

I've met so many founders who, after one good trade fair or a viral reel, feel the pressure to "go big" but end up burning out, breaking systems that were actually working, or distancing themselves from the very product that made them successful.

Here's what I've learned: growth is not about doing more, it's about doing what works more often, more consistently, and with more clarity.

The Panipat Family Exporter: From Chaos to Clarity

A Real Case Study

The Background

Ravi, a second-generation rug exporter based in Panipat, inherited a loyal customer base and a deep understanding of textiles. His business had solid demand, especially from international buyers who trusted his family's reputation. Yet behind the scenes, the operations were anything but smooth.

"We were working 12 hours a day but still felt behind," Ravi recalls. Delays in dispatch, inconsistent costing, and last-minute firefighting had become routine. Most of the decision-making was based on gut instinct, scattered notes, and memory. Despite their efforts, errors were frequent, and the team often found themselves scrambling to correct avoidable mistakes.

The Challenge

The core issues included:

- Inaccurate or outdated costing sheets
- No standardized tracking for dispatch readiness
- Quality control and sampling were handled verbally, with no visual record
- Increasing pressure from buyers for faster responses and greater transparency

Ravi's team had the expertise but lacked structure. The business was running on experience, not systems.

The Transformation

With guidance and a shift in mindset, Ravi implemented just three key digital systems, all simple, low-cost, and easy to maintain:

1. **Centralized Product Master:** A single, organized Google Sheet that held all core product details: SKUs, sizes, materials, prices, and photos, accessible to everyone in the team.
2. **Dispatch Checklist:** A standardized pre-shipment checklist to ensure nothing slipped through the cracks, from labeling and documentation to final QC and packaging.
3. **QC Photo Library:** A shared drive organized by the client and PO, where final product photos were uploaded before dispatch, giving buyers visual confirmation and building trust.

The Amazing Results

- 90% reduction in dispatch errors
- Faster internal coordination, as every team member referred to the same product and process documents
- Improved buyer confidence, one European client even commented:

  "You guys are now more professional than half the brands in Germany."
- Doubled order volume with less than half the stress

The Lesson

You don't need complex software to look and operate like a world-class business. Ravi's transformation came not from spending more, but from organizing better. Simple systems, implemented consistently, created clarity where there was once chaos.

The Global Handmade Market in 2025 and Beyond

If you're reading this book, it's because you believe in the future of handmade rugs. But belief without awareness can still leave you stuck.

Now that your most common myths have been busted, it's time to move forward. To grow smart, you need to understand where the global handmade market is headed.

- **The good news?** The opportunity is bigger than ever.
- **The challenge?** Only the businesses that align with the new buyer's expectations will win.

The Buyer Has Changed

The rug buyer of 2025 is not the same as the rug buyer of 2005. Back then, bulk orders through trade shows and long-standing importers were the norm. Today's buyer is younger, faster, more digitally connected, and more conscious.

- **Transparency is expected, not optional.** A growing share of buyers want to know: Who made this rug? Were they paid fairly? Was it child-labor-free?
- **Sustainability sells.** Europe and North America are seeing regulations and consumer pressure around eco-friendly products. Brands that can't show sustainability are at risk of being left behind.
- **Design + Story = Premium.** In a sea of rugs, the ones that tell a compelling story command higher margins.

Handmade vs. Machine-Made: The Perception Shift

Machine-made rugs dominate based only on price. They're fast, cheap, and uniform. But in 2025, buyers aren't choosing machine-made to save money; they're choosing handmade to save meaning.

Your job isn't to compete on price. It's to position handmade rugs as art with utility; products that carry heritage, emotion, and authenticity that no machine can replicate. Shared below are certain opportunity areas that you can begin tapping into-

Market Opportunity Pockets

1. **Boutique Hospitality:** Hotels, cafes, and co-working spaces increasingly seek unique, story-driven rugs to differentiate their interiors.
2. **Direct-to-Consumer E-Commerce:** Niche interior platforms, subscription-based home decor boxes, and Shopify-powered brands are growing.

3. **Conscious Luxury Buyers:** Scandinavian markets, Japan, and certain U.S. cities are leading the demand for sustainable, minimalistic, story-rich rugs.
4. **Interior Designers & Architects:** Small studios now rely on artisan collectives and boutique exporters to provide traceable, customizable products.

A Simple Future Lens Checklist

If you want to keep up your legacy, you need to move with the market and future-proof your business.

Before you pitch your next client or launch your next SKU, ask yourself:

- Is my product sustainable?
- Is my process traceable?
- Is my client digital-first?
- Is my story clear and repeatable?

If you can confidently answer "yes" to these four, you're not just ready for the future, you're already ahead of 80% of the industry.

Your Key Takeaways

- **The Handmade-Rug Market is Full of Opportunities;** all you have to do is align yourself.
- **Digital is not complex; disorganized is.** The biggest myth holding your business back is that digital transformation is only for big companies. In reality, free tools like Google Sheets can bring massive clarity and control without a tech team.
- **The mindset shift matters more than the money shift.** You don't need a big loan or a new office to grow. You need

to replace guesswork with visibility and turn processes into repeatable systems.

- **Growth doesn't require you to change everything.** You just need to consistently do the right things, better, and more often.
- **Real results come from small systems done well.** Your transformation doesn't start with spending. It starts with simplifying.

CHAPTER 2

From Chaos to Clarity

Solving the Real Problems Holding You Back

In your mind, you may perhaps be still asking yourself, "Why should I listen to this guy?" Maybe you already follow a few Instagram rug sellers. Maybe you've heard consultants pitch fancy software. But here's the loop: Most people talk about growth without ever showing you the foundation.

I've been through what you're going through: cancelled orders, unpaid clients, clueless teams, pricing confusions, vendor misfires, and logistics nightmares.

I didn't just learn strategies, I built them inside the mess.

When our export client went bankrupt and left us with ₹80 lakh of stock, we didn't sink. We adapted. We built a barcode-based fulfillment model. We sold directly. We pivoted to Shopify. And it worked.

This book is not theory: It's an applied survival and success strategy.

I show you how to use tools that cost nothing but return everything. I don't just show you how to build SOPs, but to simplify the chaos. **Because I come from a world where every rupee saved is a rupee earned.** I know you're tired of being reactive and finally want to become predictable. Profitable. Peaceful.

This book is not a shortcut. It's a field-tested navigation system, and I'm just the fellow artisan who's already walked a few miles ahead, ready to shine a torch for you.

In the previous chapter, we began by busting the biggest, most common, and costliest myth in our industry.

In this chapter, we will discuss the top 3 problems that trap most Rugpreneurs and how to avoid or manage them.

Problem 1: "I sent the sample, but they never ordered."

This is a heartbreak most of us have experienced. You invest time, money, and emotion in creating the perfect piece. You pack it carefully. You follow up for weeks. And then silence.

What went wrong?

Often, it's not your rug. It's the buyer's confusion.

- They forgot your rates.
- They showed it to their client without specs.
- They couldn't explain how it's priced or made.

When there's no system, even your best product gets lost in translation.

The Solution:

- Never send a sample without a clear visual reference, specs, price band, and reorder code.
- After dispatch, set a structured follow-up loop, not nagging, but nurturing.
- A reminder with images.
- A follow-up mail with 2 line item suggestions.

This isn't sales. It's memory management, for both you and them.

The Real Case of The Bhadohi Manufacturer

Turning a 'No' into A ₹42 Lakh Order

The Background

Based in Bhadohi, one of India's most prominent rug-producing hubs, this manufacturer had scale, skill, and a strong product portfolio. Their team was confident when a large Spanish buyer visited the factory; the sampling had gone well, and interest was high. But things didn't go as expected.

Despite liking the product, the buyer walked away. The feedback was blunt but honest:

"There's no proper documentation, no QC system, and the costing is unclear."

Months of sampling, communication, and relationship-building fell apart in minutes. The rejection was not because of the product, but because of the lack of professionalism in the process.

The Challenge

This was a classic case of strong operations in the workshop, but weak systems in the office. The manufacturer lacked:

- A polished catalog with technical specs
- A transparent costing structure that could be shared with clients
- A system to manage purchase orders or show quality control protocols

In today's B2B world, a product alone isn't enough. Buyers need confidence in your ability to deliver cleanly, clearly, and repeatedly.

The Transformation

We worked with the Bhadohi team to build a client-ready system using everyday tools, no expensive software, just clarity and structure:

1. **Pitch-Ready Catalog with QR-Linked Specs:** A clean, visual catalog where every product had a QR code linking to a digital spec sheet, including size, material, lead time, and care instructions.
2. **Purchase Order Workflow:** A clear system to receive, confirm, and track POs, with milestone-based updates for the buyer.

3. **Backend Costing Framework:** A structured sheet to map raw material, labor, margin, and logistics costs, making it easy to quote transparently and accurately.

The Amazing Results

Three months later, the same Spanish client returned, this time to a completely different experience.

- Impressed by the professionalism and clarity, they placed a ₹42 lakh order within 4 days, with a 10% advance payment upfront.
- A cold lead turned warm again and closed fast
- The team regained confidence in pitching globally
- Processes are now in place to handle more clients with similar expectations

The Lesson

You rarely get a second chance in exports, but when you do, preparation pays off. For this Bhadohi manufacturer, transforming their backend systems didn't just win them a deal; it changed how they show up in the global market.

Problem 2: "Clients always ask for discounts. They don't understand my costs."

It's not that clients want to cheat you.

They simply don't see what you see.

- To them, a 5x8 rug is a number.

- They don't know the cotton came from Panipat
- The dyeing was done twice,
- The finishing took 6 hours by hand.

The Solution:

The shift here is not price: **it's perception.**

- Break your cost into 3–4 clean parts when you explain: base material, process, finish, handling.
- If needed, give an estimated artisan wage per piece.
- The more confident you are in your breakup, the less likely they are to question the total.

Transparency is not weakness: it's power.

Problem 3: "My business is running, but I feel exhausted and still unsure if I'm growing."

This is the invisible trap.

- Revenue comes in.
- Work is happening.
- But you feel like you're always chasing.
- You don't know your margin per SKU.
- You can't delegate.

You're reacting, not leading.

The Solution:

Begin with a very simple exercise: make your business visible on one sheet of paper.

- One column for Products.
- One for Costs. One for Clients.
- One for Orders.
- If it can't be seen, it can't be scaled.

Visibility creates calm. And calm creates creativity, the real muscle that built your business in the first place.

Digital Storytelling That Sells

Let's face it: the answer to all the problems stated above could be a simple story that shifts the perception around your product and kills most, if not all, objections.

A rug without a story is just fabric on the floor.

However, a rug with a story becomes a conversation piece, an identity marker, a memory.

Storytelling is no longer "nice to have".

It's how you cut through noise, justify your pricing, and build trust in an instant.

The Power of Origin

Every handmade rug carries a history: the artisan's skill, the local dyeing process, the cultural motif. Yet most businesses never share these details with buyers. When you communicate the why and how of your rug, you elevate it from product to heritage.

A Simple Storytelling Formula

- **Origin:** Where does the idea come from? (Ex: inspired by Jaipur's stepwells)
- **Process:** How was it made? (Ex: 14 days of hand-tufting by three artisans)
- **People:** Who's behind it? (Ex: Meet Anita, our dyeing specialist)
- **Promise:** Why should the buyer care? (Ex: Each purchase funds artisan education)

Remember, A Short-Form Video = Long-Term Trust

Platforms like Instagram Reels, YouTube Shorts, and even WhatsApp broadcast lists are the fastest way to build credibility.

A 20-second video of an artisan knotting yarn speaks louder than any catalog PDF.

Build Your Rug Story Bank

Here are 10 story suggestions every rug business should record once and reuse forever:

1. ✓Artisan at the loom
2. ✓Natural dyeing in process
3. ✓QC and dispatch behind-the-scenes
4. ✓Rug being rolled for shipping
5. ✓Artisan interview (their journey)
6. ✓Raw materials being prepared
7. ✓Custom design sketch to final rug
8. ✓Team packaging with care notes
9. ✓Buyer unboxing video (with permission)
10. ✓Founder sharing the mission in their own words

One strong story doesn't just sell a rug; it builds a brand.

Your Key Takeaways

- You don't need a 20-person tech team.
- You need clarity.
- And a willingness to learn.
- Storytelling kills objections & builds brands.

When you solve the right problems, not the surface ones, but the ones that steal your peace, your business begins to run like a rhythm, not a reaction.

CHAPTER 3

Overcoming Emotional Heartbreaks With Practical Systems

Heart Break 1. The Rejection That Stings, and Teaches

Every rug seller has faced it:

- You nurture a potential client
- Answer every question
- Quote your best rate,
- And just when you think the deal is about to close, they vanish. Or worse, they come back saying, "We found something cheaper."

That sting isn't just about money. It's about value.

It makes you question your worth, your pricing, and your product.

But here's the truth: rejection is not always about you.

- Sometimes, it's about timing.
- Sometimes, it's about how clearly you communicated your difference.

- And sometimes, it's about the buyer not being ready for your kind of product.

Here's what to do:

Instead of getting bitter, get better.

After a rejection, review:

- Did they really understand what made your rug different?
- Did they receive a story, a sample, or just a price?
- Did you follow up with clarity, or did you vanish, too?
- The key isn't to chase every buyer. It's to filter better, educate deeper, and nurture longer.

Sometimes the ones who say "no" now come back six months later, if you've stayed present in their mind.

Heartbreak 2. The Return That Feels Like Failure

Returns hurt more than cancellations.

Because you fulfilled, you shipped, and you believed it was done.

Then you hear: "Rug has color bleeding" or "Not as expected." It shakes your confidence.

But most returns aren't about product failure.

They're about expectation mismatch.

Here's what to do:

- Always document your product specs clearly, give disclaimers where necessary: color may vary, and handmade irregularities are natural, etc.
- Share care instructions and disclaimers as part of your packaging.
- Never skip the QC photo step.
- A visual record protects your credibility.

A return is not a reflection of your failure; it's a signal to improve how you communicate what you're delivering.

Heartbreak 3. The Emotional Toll of Being the Face of the Brand

When you run a handmade rug business, you're not just the founder. You're:

- The designer
- The negotiator,
- The quality checker,
- The client manager
- The accountant
- And often, the one who loses sleep when orders go wrong.

The emotional burden is real. We don't talk enough about it.

You take things personally because you care. But that care must be balanced by boundaries. Not every client deserves a discount. Not every request is urgent. Not every late night is noble.

Here's what to do:

- Build small systems. They act as buffers.
- Delegate. Even if it's just one person handling WhatsApp or inventory.
- Take pride in saying "We're not a fit" to the wrong customer.

Protecting your energy is part of protecting your brand.

Using Sustainability as a Sales Strategy, Not a Slogan

Still stinging from the returns, we'll learn to leverage sustainability as a strategy. You've heard the word "sustainability" so often that it may sound like a marketing buzzword.

But for global buyers, it's not optional anymore; it's the deciding factor.

Here's the good news: as a handmade rug entrepreneur, you already have a head start.

Why Sustainability Matters to Buyers

- **Regulations:** The EU and U.S. are rolling out stricter import standards around ethical sourcing.
- **Conscious Consumers:** 65% of millennials say they're willing to pay more for sustainable products.
- **Brand Differentiation:** Retailers want proof of ethics and eco-friendliness because their buyers demand it.

Show, Don't Tell

You don't need million-rupee certifications to prove sustainability. You need visible proof. Examples:

- **Artisan Wage Cards:** Share a simple card that says: "This rug supported 3 artisans over 10 days of work."
- **Traceability via QR Codes:** Print a QR code on the rug tag that links to a short video or page about the making process.
- **Eco-Dyeing Stories:** Capture your natural dyeing process and share it online.
- **Care Notes:** Add a note in the packaging that highlights natural materials and responsible processes.

A Real-World Example

A Mirzapur-based brand once struggled to land Scandinavian buyers despite strong quality. The breakthrough came **when they began including artisan stories and natural dyeing videos with every catalog.**

Within 6 months, they signed a partnership with a boutique chain in Sweden, not because their rugs were cheaper, but because their sustainability proof was visible.

5 Sustainability Proofs You Can Show Without Spending Lakhs

1. ✓Artisan interview videos (free, authentic, powerful)
2. ✓Dyeing process transparency (photos or short clips)
3. ✓Wage transparency (approximate, not exact salaries)
4. ✓QR-linked spec sheets showing origin and process
5. ✓Packaging notes highlighting eco materials

Remember: buyers don't just want to buy rugs; they want to buy responsibility.

Your Key Takeaways

- Rejections teach resilience.
- Returns sharpen your delivery.
- Emotional setbacks force you to create systems.
- You're not just building a rug brand, you're building emotional durability. The kind that keeps you grounded through chaos and clear-headed through growth.
- Make sustainability your sales strategy, not just a slogan.

CHAPTER 4

The Silent Killer: Growth Without Repeatability

Imagine this: you bag a huge order from a new buyer. You accept it with pride.

But then you realize:

- ➢ You don't have a confirmed costing for that SKU
- ➢ Artisan availability is unclear
- ➢ You're unsure whether the raw material is in stock
- ➢ You've committed to a dispatch date based on emotion, not capacity
- ➢ Now your team is in panic mode. You skip QC. You ship in a hurry.

The rugs return. The client is disappointed. And worse, your confidence takes a hit.

This isn't a failure of growth. It's a failure of repeatable systems.

The Solution: Scale Like a Studio, Not a Factory

Scaling doesn't mean doubling your SKUs or staff.

It means:

- **Locking your core collection:** 10–15 SKUs you can deliver blindfolded. These become your hero products.
- **Tightening your fulfillment rhythm:** Know how long each stage takes, not in theory, but in lived reality.
- **Automating what repeats:** Every dispatch email, cost sheet format, and packing label doesn't need reinvention.

You don't have to stop customizing. Just don't build your entire business on exceptions. Build it on excellence.

A Bonus Tip: Leave Space for Magic, But Plan for Chaos

The handmade industry thrives on creative chaos: color swatches evolve, textures shift, and ideas come at 11.00 p.m. That's part of the charm.

But your backend shouldn't mirror this chaos.

Have creative freedom in the front, but operational clarity in the back.

That's how you protect your team, impress your clients, and preserve your joy.

A Jaipur Women-Led Design Studio: From Handmade to High-End

A Real Case Study

The Background

In the heart of Jaipur, two sisters launched a boutique design studio with a clear vision: to blend India's rich textile heritage with modern design sensibilities. Their handmade rugs and textiles stood out for their aesthetics, craftsmanship, and originality. But behind the creative success was an operational struggle.

Despite growing interest from international buyers, the studio struggled with backend execution. Sample specifications were lost, artisan timelines were vague, and production delays became a recurring issue. A turning point came when they missed a bulk shipment deadline for a major Paris-based client, damaging trust and nearly costing them the account.

The Challenge

The studio's key pain points included:

- No centralized system for managing samples and specs
- Inconsistent artisan coordination and follow-ups
- No real-time view of production status
- Difficulty scaling without losing control over timelines and quality

Creative brilliance was not enough; they needed structure to support growth and reliability.

The Transformation

We helped the team implement a basic but powerful ERP-like setup using free Google tools, no software purchases, no consultants, no IT team.

The key systems included:

1. **Live Costing Sheet:** A dynamic sheet that auto-updates input prices, sampling costs, and profit margins, giving instant clarity on every product's financials.
2. **Artisan Calendar:** A simple but effective production planner that mapped artisan capacity, timelines, and material flow, ensuring no bottlenecks or missed handovers.
3. **Sample Status Dashboard:** A real-time dashboard tracking the progress of each sample, from design brief to dispatch, improving visibility and accountability across the board.

The Amazing Results

- On-time fulfillment of their next large PO
- Improved trust with buyers due to transparent timelines and regular updates
- Featured in a niche European interiors blog, praised for their "*traceable and thoughtful production story*"
- Better workload management and team morale, thanks to fewer last-minute crises

The Lesson

Structure empowers creativity. For this women-led studio, simple digital workflows turned their backend from a blind spot into a competitive advantage. Their story is proof that handmade can still be high-end when supported by the right systems.

Building Partnerships, Not Just Clients

A common mistake in the rug business is chasing endless one-time clients. This leads to burnout and unpredictable cash flow. The smarter play? Build partnerships.

The Difference

- A client buys a rug.
- A partner builds a collection with you, trusts your systems, and returns year after year.

How to Turn Clients Into Partners

- **Exclusive Collections:** Offer a set of SKUs only available to one client. This builds loyalty.
- **Follow-Up Structure:** Don't just deliver. Follow up after 30 days with reorder suggestions or new designs.
- **Co-Branded Storytelling:** Share their brand's story alongside yours; show collaboration.
- **Consistency in Communication:** Simple CRMs (even a Google Sheet) with reminder dates ensure you don't vanish after an order.

Partnerships compound. One strong partner can sustain your business better than ten one-off clients.

Your Key Takeaways

Growth is not the reward for being busy; it's the result of being intentional.

- You don't need to grow faster.
- You need to grow steadier.
- Not bigger, but braver, in saying no to distractions and yes to systems that free you to be creative again.
- Build partnerships, not just clients.

The ability to repeat your excellence without fail based on systems that leave room for creativity is true growth.

CHAPTER 5

The Road Ahead: Systems, Soul & Staying Power

You've made it to the end, but really, this is the beginning.

This book was never just about systems, tools, or tips. It's about giving yourself permission to dream bigger, act smarter, and lead your rug business into the future without losing the soul of what makes it handmade.

You now understand the cost of chaos, the myths that keep us stuck, and the invisible traps that steal peace and profit.

- You've seen how artisans, studio founders, and exporters across India, from Panipat to Bhadohi, have turned their operations around with clarity, structure, and simple digital systems.
- You've seen that you don't need big teams or big budgets, you need big intent and the right foundation. And most importantly, you've realized that you are not alone in this journey.

I've been in your shoes, chasing POs, managing client drama, second-guessing costs, and wondering if growth will ever feel peaceful. What changed my path wasn't luck. It was **mindset + method.**

Building a Legacy That Lasts Beyond You

Systems give you profit. Branding gives you presence. But legacy, that gives you permanence.

If you've made it this far into the book, you already know how to survive, scale, and succeed. But here's the deeper question: **what will remain when you step away from the loom, the laptop, or the ledger?**

Most entrepreneurs think in terms of orders, quarters, or, at best, a 5-year plan. Very few think about 30 years down the line. Yet the true test of a handmade rug business isn't how many rugs you sold this year, it's whether the craft, the artisans, and the values you stood for will still stand long after you.

From Business Owner to Legacy Builder

Ask yourself: **Am I just selling rugs, or am I shaping culture?**

- When you pay an artisan fairly, you're not just closing payroll, you're funding a child's education, sustaining a skill, and preserving dignity.
- When you adopt sustainable processes, you're not just pleasing a client, you're protecting water, soil, and air for the next generation.
- When you create a brand story that respects tradition, you're not just marketing, you're safeguarding heritage against extinction.

Legacy is built in the small, everyday choices.

Documenting Your Systems-Playbook

One of the most overlooked parts of legacy-building is documentation. Too many family businesses collapse because knowledge lives only in the founder's head.

If you want your rug business to outlast you:

- Write down your costing formulas.
- Record your artisan rosters and their strengths.
- Save your best client emails and pitches as templates.
- Build a "founder's manual" that future generations or successors can use.

Your goal is simple: make your business **transferable,** whether to your children, a professional team, or even a future buyer.

Mentorship as Multiplication

Legacy isn't only about what you leave behind; it's also about who you lift along the way. The handmade rug industry suffers because too many of us play in isolation. But imagine if every successful rugpreneur mentored five more. **The impact would multiply across villages, cities, and countries.**

Mentorship doesn't need to be formal. It could be as simple as:

- Sharing your system templates with another small exporter.
- Coaching one artisan to become an independent entrepreneur.
- Hosting an internship for design students to learn heritage crafts.

Your knowledge has compounding power. Don't hoard it. Share it.

Turning a Rug Business Into a Global Brand

When you look at the world's most admired legacy brands, from Japanese kimono houses to Italian leather ateliers, they all have one thing in common: **they built a story bigger than themselves.**

For your rug business, this could mean:

- Creating collections that showcase Indian craft at international design fairs.
- Partnering with global NGOs or sustainability forums to highlight artisan empowerment.
- Building a digital museum of your designs and processes for the world to learn from.

A rug brand that ties heritage with global vision doesn't just make sales, it makes history.

A Personal Note: Why Legacy Matters to Me

When I look back at my own journey, I see the faces of artisans who trusted me, buyers who bet on me, and family who believed in me. The revenue numbers are important, yes. But the real pride comes from knowing that 500+ artisans doubled their income, rural women got employment, and our craft traveled to 43+ countries because we chose systems and soul over shortcuts.

That's legacy. It's not mine alone; it belongs to every artisan, every customer, every partner who walked the path with me.

So, as you turn this final page, I invite you to ask yourself:

- What will my rug business stand for in 20 years from now?
- Whose lives will it have changed?

- Will it vanish when I retire, or will it breathe life into generations ahead?

Legacy is not built on a single sale or even a single system. It is built when your values, your processes, and your people align to create something timeless.

This book gave you the blueprint for systems. Now it's your turn to add soul and scale it into a legacy.

The rugs you weave are not just for today's floors. They are for tomorrow's stories.

Go build that legacy.

Now the blueprint is in your hands.

This isn't the end of the road: this is the launchpad.

If something inside you is saying, "I'm ready to take this seriously", then I invite you to step into the next phase with me.

Let's Take the Next Step Together

Book a Free Discovery Call

If you want personal help applying these systems to your business, book a 1:1 session with me. Let's map your next move: www.theamitjain.com

Download the Rugpreneur Toolkit

Ready-to-use templates, sample trackers, costing formats, and dispatch checklists — the same ones we use.

www.theamitjain.com/tools

Join the Webinar Waitlist

Be the first to know when I run my live training sessions and deep-dive walkthroughs.

www.theamitjain.com/webinar

Subscribe for Weekly Rugpreneur Tips

Short, actionable insights sent directly to your inbox to help you stay sharp and ahead.

www.theamitjain.com/newsletter

Let's build. Let's lead. Let's leave a legacy, one system at a time.

About the Author

Amit Jain is not just an exporter; he's a system builder, a second-generation entrepreneur, and a storyteller of Indian excellence. As Managing Director of Weavinghands Rugs Pvt. Ltd. (formerly Shree Sai International), Amit leads one of India's most process-driven rug export firms, known for combining traditional craftsmanship with cutting-edge operational clarity.

Born in Mirzapur, Amit has been instrumental in helping over 200 international buyers, from boutique designers to large-scale retailers, confidently source high-quality, handmade rugs from India. His approach goes beyond product: he helps clients trust the process. His ERP systems, live production tracking workflows, and design-to-dispatch visibility models have transformed how artisans and agents work together.

He is also the creator of the Rugpreneur Toolkit: a step-by-step framework that enables fellow Indian exporters to implement practical tools like costing sheets, PO templates, product masters, and dispatch trackers without expensive software or foreign consultants.

Through coaching, speaking, and writing, Amit is helping redefine what it means to be a successful Indian exporter in the modern era, someone who leads with culture, competes with clarity, and scales without losing soul.

When he's not designing ERP sheets or mentoring young entrepreneurs, you'll find him learning, reading, or dreaming about a better export ecosystem for all.

Explore his tools, templates, and more at: www.theamitjain.com